The Healing Power of
Dreams

A Spiritual Process of Opening, Unfolding, and Evolving

Barb Smith

BALBOA.
PRESS
A DIVISION OF HAY HOUSE

Balboa Press books may be ordered through booksellers or by contacting:

Balboa Press
A Division of Hay House
1663 Liberty Drive
Bloomington, IN 47403
www.balboapress.com
1 (877) 407-4847

Because of the dynamic nature of the Internet, any web addresses or
links contained in this book may have changed since publication and
may no longer be valid. The views expressed in this work are solely those
of the author and do not necessarily reflect the views of the publisher,
and the publisher hereby disclaims any responsibility for them.

The author of this book does not dispense medical advice or prescribe the use
of any technique as a form of treatment for physical, emotional, or medical
problems without the advice of a physician, either directly or indirectly. The
intent of the author is only to offer information of a general nature to help
you in your quest for emotional and spiritual well-being. In the event you use
any of the information in this book for yourself, which is your constitutional
right, the author and the publisher assume no responsibility for your actions.

Any people depicted in stock imagery provided by Thinkstock are models,
and such images are being used for illustrative purposes only.
Certain stock imagery © Thinkstock.

Printed in the United States of America.

ISBN: 978-1-4525-1576-2 (sc)
ISBN: 978-1-4525-1578-6 (hc)
ISBN: 978-1-4525-1577-9 (e)

Library of Congress Control Number: 2014909607

Balboa Press rev. date: 6/4/2014

Contents

Dedication

I dedicate this book to my family, to my beloved husband Dave who is always very supportive, loving, and caring, and to my two beautiful daughters Sarah and Megan. May your lives be filled with infinite love, joy, and blessings. My wish for you will always be a life full of love and happiness, a gift you've given me.

Preface by Barb Smith

The writings in this book are not based on scientific proof but rather meaningful experiences and events in my life. I am not a doctor or a scientist, and I don't profess to be a doctor or a scientist of any kind. My life experiences gifted me with profound insight and wisdom, revealing why things happened the way they did, and why they happened. *"Everything Happens for A Reason"* is one of my favorite mantras. Quite often while being caught up in the drama of the experience we can't see the forest for the trees. It is in hind sight that it all falls into place, making more sense to us. Life's experiences and lessons are what help us gain more wisdom and insight, learn and grow, and become more of who we are truly meant to be. It is this process of opening, unfolding, and evolving that leads us to our true authentic self. By going within, surrendering and letting go, there is more room to receive, to receive more love, more grace, and more blessings. Solutions and profound insights are waiting to be discovered in this adventure we call life, and it is through my experiences I have discovered who I truly am, my true authentic self. I am what I am because of my experiences. I AM what I AM.

Note from the Author

Family is one of God's greatest masterpieces. The key to a successful and happy life is to keep family members close to your heart and part of your life each and every day. Family is by chance not by choice but by choosing unconditional love you can create your own beautiful dream instead of destroying everything around you. Living a life full of joy and unconditional love every day is living the dream, and creating Heaven here on Earth. When you unlock the immense power of love, you will see everything through the eyes of love. Love is what you are made of. Love is the answer. Every time you choose love, you are lighting up the world. Your family is part of your life for a reason. At times you are the teacher, other times the student depending on the lessons that need to be learned. Family and their dynamics are there to assist us in bringing out those qualities and experiences that need to be attained in order to grow, evolve, and become that great magnificent being you are meant to be. Writing this self-help memoir is honoring my soul, and my message of love. Love is the greatest gift of all. Love heals all. I choose love! What do you choose?

Introduction

JOURNEY OF SELF-DISCOVERY

The most difficult thing in my life was to get to know my true self. The writings in this book are a journey of my self-discovery, a journey that once it began everything seemed brighter, lighter, and more loving. It is through this book that I hope to inspire you to find your inner wealth, to conceivably discover who you are truly meant to be. Perhaps through your journey of self-discovery, you may inspire others to find their inner wealth as well.

> *"If your actions inspire others to dream more, learn more, do more and become more, you are a leader."* John Quincy Adams

As my life began to unfold and reveal more of its hidden treasures to me, that's when I realized that a handful of nails were preventing me from growing and evolving but once my hands were open to receive other things, no longer was I solving my problem with a hammer. To understand everything, is to forgive everything. Things are neither good nor bad; judgement of the thing makes it so. I needed to change the way I saw things in order to receive what I wanted, what I was looking for. Fear and anger dissolved away once I had a clearer understanding of my life and why things happened the way they did. Soon everything became transparent.

A successful life is when you can look back and see the mountains you have climbed; feel great gratitude and joy for all your accomplishments; and be proud of every minute and every decision you made along the way. Life isn't measured by what you have but more of what you have accomplished; the obstacles of which you overcame, and the people you've inspired or helped along the way.

> *"Dreams are today's answers to tomorrow's questions."* Edgar Cayce

Much like the lyrics in John Newton's song called Amazing Grace, I once was lost but now I'm found, was blind but now I see. I can clearly see what I didn't see before. Fear and anger dissolved away exposing the hidden treasures of my soul.

> *"Amazing Grace, how sweet the sound,*
> *That saved a wretch like me.*
> *I once was lost but now am found,*
> *Was blind, but now I see."*

Dream healing, what I call healing through dreams, gave me clarity and profound insights. It inspired me, guided me, and encouraged me along my path to becoming a greater person, a person full of unconditional love for all, all life, and all beings. We are all meant to become great magnificent beings, and live a life of Heaven here on Earth, and through dream healing I believe this is possible, for everyone.

PART I

Remembering and Understanding

Chapter One

DREAM HEALING

Do you want clarity in your life? Are you ready for healthy loving relationships? Do you want your life to flow with ease and grace? You are an infinite being and can live a life of calm and peace. If heaven is a state of mind, not a location, wouldn't you want to create Heaven here on Earth?

Once you understand how dream healing can transform your life, you can live a life of Heaven here on Earth.

> *"Create a Beautiful Dream. Your word can create the most beautiful dream, or your word can destroy everything around you. Impeccability of the word creates beauty, love, and Heaven on Earth."* Don Miguel Ruiz, The Four Agreements.

Dream Healing is a spiritual process of opening, unfolding and evolving much like the lotus flower. The lotus flower is beautiful and full of life, and it inspires us to strive through difficulties. It springs forth beautiful blooms from the murky darkness at the bottom of the pond. As the lotus flower opens its petals, it reveals more beauty and so too can your beautiful soul through dream healing.

You can transform and heal your life through analyzing and understanding your dream messages. When you are open to receive messages through your dreams, you can heal and transform your life in several ways. As you do your life begins to unfold, exposing more aspects of you that you didn't know existed, and as a result you begin evolving as a spiritual being, your true-self, and your soul's purpose will then be revealed to you.

Dreams are a catalyst in manifesting, and can assist in balancing your mind, body and spirit. You can heal yourself and others spiritually, physically, and mentally through dream healing. In the dream state you have access to significant information that may not be available to you when awake. Your dream is much like a window, an opening to your subconscious which can reveal to you answers and your secret desires. You may not even realize how you truly feel about something until you experience it in your dream state. By tapping into this window of clarity, you can gain relevant knowledge and wisdom and discover more aspects of yourself that you didn't know existed.

> Job 33:15 (Kings James version) *"In a dream in a vision of the night when deep sleep falleth upon men, in slumberings upon the bed; then he openeth the ears of men and seals their instructions."*

Dreams are full of messages and symbols that give insight and understanding of various situations or conflicts you may be experiencing in your life. A dream can give you courage and confidence to face your fear and to confront your issues or struggles head on. Your dream is your message. It is unique to you and reflects any struggles or challenges that you may be going through at the present time. Your dreams encapsulate your perception, your feelings, and your thoughts. Every aspect of your dream is important and valuable, even if it may seem minute and insignificant at the time. Various symbols or images may trigger a feeling or a memory. There are many resources available out there that will help you analyze and interpret your dreams and their messages. There have been many books written on the subject and many internet resources available as well. Noted at the end of this book are just some of those resources available to you. When analyzing your dream, always consider what your feelings are. How did that dream make you feel? Were you afraid or angry? Did you feel abundantly loved and full of joy? Or did you receive an answer to a question or a situation you are currently going through?

An example of this would be if you have a dream of lots of snakes wiggling and crawling all around you. Snakes may signify hidden fears or worries, or that someone or some people in your life are being callous, ruthless and can't be trusted. The positive symbol of seeing snakes in a dream signifies healing, transformation, knowledge and wisdom. So then you need to ask yourself, what were your feelings during the dream? Were you afraid of the snakes? Or were you completely calm and unaffected by the snakes surrounding you? If you weren't afraid of the snakes in your dream but you are in real life, the dream would suggest that there is great healing, transformation, knowledge and wisdom surrounding you in life.

Strong and insightful messages come through while dreaming, in your dream state. Through dreams you can access higher wisdom; higher aspects of yourself; qualities and aspects of yourself that you didn't know existed. When you do, you understand your soul's purpose and receive answers or solutions to problems or issues you are experiencing in your life.

Remembering and understanding your dreams is the key to begin the process of healing. Analyzing and understanding the messages is when a healing begins. At times it may be difficult to fully understand how the dream message relates to what's happening in your life. When this happens you may be shown the same specific message but in different dream scenarios. You will continue to receive dreams with the same message but presented in a different way, a way that you may understand more easily, until you fully understand its message, or the conflict has been resolved in your life.

An example of same themed dreams would be if you were grocery shopping at your local grocery store. You are pushing your shopping cart along, putting groceries in your cart and then suddenly you realize that you are naked, completely nude, and not a stitch of clothing on you. You feel embarrassed and mortified, and immediately want to leave the store before someone sees you standing there completely and absolutely naked. Another scenario but with the same dream message would be if you were at your workplace standing before a group of your peers presenting a topic of interest and then all of a sudden you realize that you are standing in front of everyone naked, completely nude, and not a stitch of clothing on you. You feel embarrassed and mortified, and you just want to leave before someone notices that you're not wearing any clothes. Both scenarios carry the same message. The dream message here means that you are feeling vulnerable and may be hiding something or are afraid that others can see right through you, since metaphorically clothes are a means of concealment. You are fearful of being exposed, or ridiculed, or disgraced about something. Or it may mean that you feel that all eyes are on you no matter where you go, whether it's to the grocery store or at the workplace. In both dream scenarios no one noticed that you were naked which means that your fears were unfounded, no one noticed except you.

Chapter Two

YOU ARE PERFECT!

What if you were told that you were and are never broken, never diminished, and never wrong? Wouldn't that be the most liberating statement to resonate within your being? Every situation, every choice you've made, every thought you've had, has made you who you are today. You are perfect the way you are. Your action is a result of your experiences and your action will gift you with healing.

The true test is how you handle life's experiences. Do you handle them with love and grace, or are you bitter and angry? Healing is the way to your true authentic self. Feelings and emotions can imprison you if you allow them to prevent you from learning and growing. The key is to observe and acknowledge your emotions with calm and ease, and then freely let them go. Release them freely. You are not your feelings. You are the one experiencing them. Through this book you'll find ways of releasing those emotions so that you can live a life free and ready for the next adventure. Love continues to flow freely with an open heart, a heart free of anger, bitterness, and fear. Wouldn't you want to live a life full of love and grace? What a beautiful life it can be!

Life is full of bumps, turns, and surprises but as you experience these you are learning, growing, and becoming more of who you are truly meant to be, your true authentic self. You are evolving into the most magnificent person you were meant to be. The better you know and understand yourself, the clearer your purpose becomes and soon you'll be able to see every opportunity or challenge as a gift, or as I like to call it a blessing. These opportunities are a chance for you to expand your greatness, become more of who you are truly meant to be. It is through this growth that you begin to see your true authentic self. As you embrace all aspects of yourself, you begin to find your inner wealth, your great magnificence. Embrace every opportunity to grow, for your soul to grow; see the blessings in every event; and by being your true authentic self you will find your inner wealth, your great magnificence.

> *"It's not the length of life; but the depth of life."*
> Ralph Waldo Emerson

Every experience in life is meant to propel you to seek greater love and to find your inner peace, your inner wealth. Inner peace comes from living your true authentic self. Trying to be someone you are not is living a false life and by doing so can prevent you from finding inner peace and greater love. Life is full of experiences and obstacles but they are a part of your life for a reason. These experiences and obstacles assist you in moving forward to becoming a greater human being, someone with more love, grace, and more compassion. As your inner wealth grows so too does your beautiful soul. Your heart begins to expand, opening wider and wider. Even more love and grace will come your way. It becomes a snowballing effect. Love attracts more love. Just like a snowball rolling down the hillside gathering and collecting more snow with every turn it takes. So too can your love. Love will attract more love, building and growing with every turn you take.

Looking at obstacles as experiences that will bring you greater joy and not seeing them as mountains or hurtles to climb over is the most essential part of bringing more joy and love into your life. Life's experiences are a part of a spiritual process of healing, and receiving blessings and gifts along the way, along your soul's path towards inner peace, towards inner wealth. Once you are able to see these challenges or obstacles as blessings, you begin to live a life full of joy, peace, and love, and begin to see everything as a blessing, a gift.

My goal is to become whole by embracing all aspects of me. All of my experiences, all of my pain, all of my joy have made me who I am today. I embrace all aspects of me. We are perfect the way we are. We are complete and we are whole when we are willing to accept this to be true. Take a look at the moon. It is always full. It's just our perspective, or our view of it, that makes it something that it's not. The moon is never just a sliver or a crescent floating in the sky. It is always full and complete, just as we are.

We have within everything that we would ever need, and once you are able to see the whole you, you will see that everything is beautiful and perfect. There is an abundance of beauty everywhere you look. I implore you. Open your eyes and your mind to see what beauty is before you.

Sometimes we don't pay attention to what's happening around us or like in the case of the moon where we think we know what we are seeing when in actuality we are only seeing part of the whole picture.

Take for instance the grains of sand under a microscope magnified 250 times are in fact beautiful multicolored, multi-shaped gems. Now you could be thinking how did I not know that? Could I have been trampling on beautiful gems without even knowing it? How is it I never thought of the moon as always being full? It's just perception, our view of the way things appear to be to us. Take another look at life around you. Are you trampling on the gems of life? Start your day and look for beauty in everything you see. Look at everything with fresh new eyes. You just may surprise yourself.

Microscope Photography Dr. Gary Greenberg,
"A Grain of Sand - Nature's Secret Wonder"
<u>http://sandgrains.com/Sand-Grains-Gallery.html</u>

Chapter Three

WHAT IS TRUE TO YOU?

To live a life full of grace, full of love, and freedom start each day with a grateful heart; live each day to the fullest and with absolute integrity; follow your joy; see blessings in everything and every event; and finish your day with a grateful heart. By being your true authentic self you will find your inner wealth, feel infinitely lighter and freer, and most of all find greater love.

Let's explore a couple of ways to test what is true to you, and what isn't. If there comes a time when you have a decision to make and you're uncertain which option to choose, try the following techniques. Not only does it demonstrate what is true and what isn't, it also demonstrates the extra strength and energy required to hold a lie, so why would you want to? Why waste your energy? Try these techniques to show what's true to you. Once you recognize with certainty the feeling you experience when something is true to you, you will no longer need to do these tests.

Technique No 1. Stand tall and straight, and vocalize a true statement. Observe how your body feels. Does it feel light or does it feel heavy? Since it is a true statement, your body should feel light and tend to lean forward in your stance.

Now test this modality by stating something that is untrue. You should feel heaviness in your body and it will tend to lean backwards, pulling away. It is similar to when you see or hear something that is displeasing to you, you will automatically pull away be leaning back, or by stepping back. Use your body as a pendulum to help choose what is right and true for you.

Technique No 2. Another way to test this is to stand tall with your arms spread out to your side shoulder high. Make a statement that is true and have someone try to press down on your arms with all their might. You will notice that you are very strong and able to resist against the pressure pushing down on your arms.

Now test this modality by making a statement that is untrue. You'll notice immediately that you are not able to resist the pressure on your arms, you become weak instantly. Again this demonstrates the extra energy that it takes to hold a lie, to hold onto something that is untrue to you. It can be harmful if you are living a life that is not of your truth.

Once you are able to determine what is true to you, what your true authentic self is, the meaning behind the dream messages will become much clearer and more significant to you. Your dreams are designed for you. They are personalized messages just for you and will help guide you along your path to inner peace, and enable you to see your blessings.

Chapter Four

THE DREAMER

The writings in this book are not based on scientific proof but rather meaningful experiences and events in my life. I am not a doctor or a scientist and I don't profess to be a doctor or a scientist of any kind. I have gained this knowledge by living and experiencing life which has given me profound insight as to why things happened the way they did, and why they happened. "Everything Happens for A Reason" is one of my favorite mantras. Quite often while being caught up in the drama of the experience we can't see the forest for the trees. It is in hind sight that it all falls into place and makes more sense to us. Life's experiences and lessons are what help us to learn and grow. It is this process of opening, unfolding, and evolving that leads us to who we are truly meant to be. Through my experiences I have discovered who I truly am. I am what I am because of my experiences. I AM what I AM.

I am a Dreamer. I have always been a dreamer. Even as a young child I recall many dreams I experienced. Soon I discovered my dreams were communicating to me. Messages, wisdom, and insight were within each and every one of them. Much to my dismay I also realized that not everyone dreams the way I do. In fact I soon discovered many don't recall their dreams at all and that's when my adventure began. I started paying more attention to my dreams, journaling and analyzing them. Dreaming has always been a part of my life and I decided that I wouldn't take them for granted. Dreams and their messages are a gift and are something that should be cherished.

Dreaming has been around for a long time. Even the scripture Job 33:15 says *"In a dream in a vision of the night when deep sleep falleth upon men, in slumberings upon the bed; then he openeth the ears of men and seals their instructions."* Messages and wisdom have been coming through our dreamscape all along. Why hadn't we known this? Perhaps we've known this but didn't believe it. I am here to tell you that there are messages in your dreams, personalized messages just for you. Once you pay attention to them and analyze them you'll be able to understand their messages and see how they can assist you in healing and transforming your life.

Many famous people were inspired by their dreams. Paul McCartney said he had the idea of "Let It Be" after a dream he had about his mother Mary during an intense period surrounding the Beatles during the "White Album". McCartney's mother passed away from cancer when he was fourteen years old. The dream inspired Paul and he said "It was great to visit with her again. I felt very blessed to have that dream. So that got me writing Let it Be". He also said in a later interview about the dream that his mother had told him "It will be all right, just let it be".

Here are a few lines from that beautiful song "Let it Be":

> *And when the broken-hearted people*
> *Living in the world agree*
> *There will be an answer*
> *Let it be*

There have been many other famous people who were inspired or received profound messages through their dreams. Abraham Lincoln dreamt of his assassination and shared his dream with his wife. Elias Howe invented the sewing machine and had received his inspiration through a dream. Jack Nicklaus finds a new golf swing in a dream. He found a new way to hold his golf club which credits to improving his golf game.

Further into this book I am going to share with you how I healed my life through understanding and analyzing my dreams. I will share with you how I overcame my biggest obstacle and how I realized that it was and is my greatest gift of all, a blessing. The insightful messages that I received through my dreams were a confirmation, a validation, and an answer to a question and a situation in my life, a question that I've been asking myself for many years. By paying attention to my dream messages I was able to heal and transform my life. I was able to find forgiveness where I thought there needn't be any.

Everyone dreams. Most people just don't recall their dreams. Through practise and exercising your dream muscle you can achieve dream recall, analyze your dreams, and receive insightful messages. I will elaborate more on this in later chapters.

A dream or even a nightmare may keep reoccurring as a way for you to work through some sort of trauma or fear. They are intended as guidance or warnings to a particular situation. For example if you dream of brakes failing on your vehicle, it might help to take a look at what's currently going on in your life, are you having a hard time slowing down? Do you need to put the brakes on something? Or it may be very important to check the actual brakes on your vehicle. Your dreams are trying to communicate a message to you and it's up to you to pay attention to them.

You may receive several dreams with the same message but with varying story lines. The dream could be trying to get a message through to you and you don't quite understand it. It could be something that you need to resolve or understand in your waking life and you will continue to receive several dreams with different story lines but with the same insightful message until you understand its message or the issue is resolved. If you don't understand your most recent dream simply request to be shown the message in a different way. The dreams will continue to come until you understand its message or the issue is resolved.

Go with your instinct when trying to analyze your dream. Your gut instinct is always your best guide. It's important to recall how you felt during the dream. What kind of emotions did you experience? Were you happy and joyful? Did what you see or experience make you feel sad or scared? You are your best dream interpreter. Go with your first instinct and pay attention to your emotions during your dream. How did the dream made you feel?

For example if you have a dream about sweeping. Sweeping can imply that you are clearing your mind of emotional and mental clutter; and that you are getting rid of all minor annoyances in your life and focusing on more important things; and that it's time to take a new stance and have a fresh outlook on life. Alternatively sweeping can mean that you are ignoring some important facts and are going against what your gut and intuition is telling you. If you are sweeping dirt under the rug it means that you are trying to cover up those annoyances and are ignoring what needs to be attended to.

In your dream if while you were sweeping the floors you felt very happy about what you were doing then it would mean that you are successfully accomplishing a task in your waking life. The dream reflects that you are working at clearing your mind of emotional and mental clutter, sweeping it all away. But alternatively if you felt worried or stressed while sweeping in your dream then it would mean that you are ignoring important facts that are going on in your life. You could be ignoring them for whatever reason. It could be out of fear. If it is fear that has you imprisoned then you will be shown dreams that reflect that fear. You may actually see yourself in prison indicating that you feel trapped, restricted and can't express yourself. As you begin to face your fears you could see yourself in a dream as a prisoner being released from prison which metaphorically means that you have overcome your fears and you will be making major changes in your waking life.

Sometimes there can be a pun or a play on words which I find rather amusing. We may not completely understand these until we are retelling or sharing our dreams with others. An example of a pun on words would be to dream about a bear. Bear symbolizes independence, the cycle of life, death and renewal, and resurrection. It also means that you are going through a period of introspection and thinking. The pun on words here is "bare", perhaps you need to bare your soul and let everything out into the open.

Quite often clear insights occur while sharing and retelling the dream to someone else. You may instantly receive additional insight to the dream when you do. There could be something further to the dream and once you speak of it, it then makes more sense to you and broadens your awareness of the situation that you are going through in your waking life. It's always helpful to share your dreams with others for this very reason. Dreams are very private and personal but if you can find a group of friends that you can trust to share your dreams with, it would be very helpful for all of you. By sharing and retelling our dreams we are helping one another to learn, grow and discover more of who we truly are. You can learn and grow through the experiences and dreams of others. For example you may have a friend retell a dream of how they were surrounded by churning water and felt they had no way out. What this dream means is that there is a lot of drama around them and they felt that they had no way of escaping. The churning of water are emotions and turmoil. Who hasn't felt like this at one time or another?

Chapter Five

TREASURES OF YOUR SOUL

Your past can not be ignored, avoided and pushed aside. It is a part of who you are. All your life experiences and lessons along the way have brought you to this point in your life. As you no longer refuse to face your past you are releasing the pain of the past and discovering the diamonds in the treasure chest of your soul. Fear will no longer control you and push your past away. Your past is a part of you, part of the complete you, your true authentic self. You are what you are because of your past and what you have experienced. Once I embraced the pain and anger of my past it dissolved away exposing the diamonds in the treasure chest of my soul. I am what I am because of my experiences and my past. I AM what I AM.

Let me share with you a dream I recall having, a dream which validates this message for me.

I was walking barefoot along a beautiful white sandy beach in a very secluded area. No one was on the beach but me. It was as though this beautiful beach was created just for me. This very peaceful and tranquil place had a beautiful white sandy shoreline and crystal clear turquoise waters. I could stay here forever, I thought to myself. It felt so heavenly. As I was walking along the sandy shore I looked down at my feet and noticed beautiful crystals in varying colors of reds, blues, purples, pinks, and greens. Some were even translucent and others were iridescent reflecting back a rainbow of colors. I had been walking on these beautiful crystals all along but hadn't even noticed them until now. I remember thinking to myself, how could I have not noticed them? As I was admiring the colorful gems, I was drawn to pick up a few. They varied in shapes and sizes, not one gem was the same. A big beautiful purple heart shaped crystal glistening and gleaming in the sunlight caught my eye. It was the most beautiful thing I had ever seen and I felted honored to hold it in my hands. I recall feeling how excited I was and how much I loved their beauty that I wanted to bring them home with me. I remember being reassured in my dream that the crystals are mine to do with what I want. They were the treasures to my soul. I was surprised. How can something so beautiful belong to me and I can do what I want with them? I was so grateful and delighted that such beauty could be mine. I decided to leave my gems on the beautiful white sandy beach where I found them so that I could come back to that location and admire them whenever I chose to. It was my private little piece of paradise where I could come to any time, a place where I could relax and admire such immense beauty. My gems, the treasures to my soul will always be there waiting for my return.

Once I was able to forgive and release the pain of my past, that's when my gems became visible to me. By pushing forward when I felt it was hopeless was the key to my success. My pain and anger dissolved away uncovering my beautiful gems, the treasures to my soul. Your gems, crystals, or gold and silver, or whatever you see as a treasure, is in your treasure chest to your soul waiting for you to discover. You could be trampling on them and not even notice just like I did until I was willing to forgive and release the pain of my past.

Microscope Photography Dr. Gary Greenberg, "A Grain of Sand - Nature's Secret Wonder" http://sandgrains. com/Sand-Grains-Gallery. html

Life is like a treasure hunt, seeking our hidden gems. Be willing to stop and see what's inside your treasure chest.

PART II

My Journey

Chapter Six

CHILDHOOD FEAR

Fear developed at a very young age for me. Fear of not being loved, fear of being unworthy of love, and fear of putting my heart out there only to have it trampled on. As a form of survival I hid this fear and retracted away from love. This lack of love was very painful and as a child I couldn't understand why I wasn't receiving love from those that meant the most to me, my family, or more specifically my mother. These feelings were buried deep inside and no one was the wiser. Living this way as a child was very painful to me and I couldn't understand why I felt so different than the rest of my family. Why did I not belong? Why did I feel that love was being withheld from me? Was I not worthy of being loved? Why did I feel this way? Why couldn't my mother love me in a way I needed? Why was love withheld from me? This enormous pain was always sitting there right on the surface waiting to be released. Any emotional event would bring up all of those emotions, all those experiences of not being loved enough, or not feeling worthy enough to be loved. Why did I not feel loved?

Why did I feel like the black sheep of the family? Why were my attitudes and perceptions so different from my family? I even recall thinking to myself, I don't even look like them physically, they all have blue eyes and I have green. Was I adopted? Was there a mix up in the hospital at birth? Why did I feel so different? Was the fact that I was so different the reason why I didn't fit in and why my family couldn't relate to me? Was I the black sheep, or was I the bright light shining in the darkness?

As a child I remember very few happy memories. Was an unhappy childhood part of the gift, part of the blessing? As a form of survival I shut myself off from my family and the rest of the world, so much so that it even hurt to be touched. It was too painful for me to be touched, emotionally and physically. If someone tried to reach out and touch me even if it was a gentle touch on my arm or my shoulder I would feel squeamish and pull away. I would think to myself this is ridiculous, why don't I want to be touched, by anyone? The world was too painful for me to experience and it was safer just to disconnect myself and look more within for my answers. I recall many times thinking that I just want to leave this world. I felt I didn't belong anywhere, and that I wasn't wanted. I was what was considered an accident and the feelings of not belonging only increased my ability to push people away. Why would I want to live, live in this world without a mother's love? Survival for me in this painful world then became avoidance of feelings and love because it was just too painful. If I couldn't receive the love I needed from the mother who brought me into this world, then I felt I wasn't deserving of love at all.

I was so good at burying my pain and keeping my emotions bottled up inside that eventually I developed severe ulcers of the stomach. Who would have thought that a child so young could have stomach ulcers? At the age of seven I was in the hospital for eleven days. The doctors ran a series of tests and were astonished when it was determined that I developed severe stomach ulcers. The doctors talked to me about my feelings and any worries I had. If they had talked to my parents about my fears and worries it hadn't made a bit of difference. There was no change in the relationship with my parents. They did not demonstrate any change in effort in showing more love for me.

Life went on as it did before except that now I had a strict diet, no greasy foods, no spicy foods, etc. I remember everyone eating pizza and pop while I sat there eating toast and taking my medicine. Things did not change in my childhood. Even at the age of eight I wanted to run away from home. I knew that I had to leave that situation in order to survive. An older sister who was sixteen at the time was going to move away and live with my grandparents. I wanted to go with her but my parents wouldn't let me. So then I wondered how I was going to get out of this situation. I was a young girl at the age of eight, probably not a good idea to run away from home so I decided to wait until I was sixteen. My plan was to move far away to a place that is sunny and warm all year round, possibly California. Age sixteen came along but then I decided it would be best if I received an education, a high school diploma so I could find a job and support myself. Age seventeen is when I graduated with a high school diploma, five months earlier than normal, and the earlier the better. I needed to leave.

Again fear was gripping me. Why didn't I have the courage to leave? Why was fear crippling me? Three months after graduation I received a job, shortly after that was the day I finally left home. I'd like to be able to say I finally had courage to face my fear and leave on my own but that wasn't the case. I was kicked out. So there I was eighteen years of age and homeless. My boyfriend at the time who is now my husband, had parents that graciously offered their couch to me until I could find a place of my own. Obviously the situation didn't change between my parents and I. There was no effort in their part to improve our situation. It was quite apparent they didn't like me or should I say that it was even more than that, they didn't love me. I actually felt that it was more than dislike that my mother had for me, it felt like hatred. So that became my quest. Why did my mother hate me so much?

Through my adolescent years I would continue to try to love others, giving love in hopes of receiving love. It seemed like if I allowed myself to love someone, I'd get hurt, every single time. So I would go about life, forcing a smile, pretending to be happy. People had no idea the pain I was feeling inside. I kept my feelings and my story to myself because I didn't want people to feel sorry for me. I didn't want them to see my pain. I didn't want sympathy, I wanted to be loved. How can I stop this hurt I feel inside. If my mother didn't love me why would anyone else? Could this lack of love also be a gift, a blessing?

At a young age I understood that sometimes life hands you lemons but it's what you do with those lemons that counts. Life isn't only about our experiences but more importantly it's how we handle those experiences. The true test is how we handle the anger and the fear. Does it consume us or do we handle our experiences with love and grace? Do I choose bitterness or do I choose love?

These experiences and feelings of not being loved, and not trusting others forced me to go within and to get to know myself, my true self. It was a true process of self-discovery. I was able to determine my goals and dreams, what I wanted out of life, and how I wanted to live. I knew I wanted to live a life full of love and joy. Throughout my whole life I always knew I could trust my inner guidance and that's how I would live my life, listening to my inner guidance and being my true authentic self. No more going through the motions of life pretending to be happy. I was going to be happy! I will be happy! I wasn't going to allow the opinions of others to make me feel sad and unwanted again. I am worthy of love! I deserve love!

Chapter Seven

MY QUEST

"In order to succeed your desire for success should be greater than your fear of failure." Bill Cosby

It was later in life I realized I had received the greatest gift I could have ever been blessed with. My quest had been answered.

I had buried anger and bitterness for another, my mother. I appeared to be happy and content on the surface but deep down inside I kept wondering what was wrong with me that I couldn't receive the love I felt I deserved, the love from a mother. Something just wasn't quite right and I spent a great deal of my life trying to understand why. Not why me but why. Why was this happening? Everyone has a sad story and I didn't share mine with others because I don't want pity, I wanted a mother's love. Very few people actually know how I truly feel inside and by writing this book and sharing my story I can hopefully help others heal their lives. I will no longer call it my sad story because it is my gift. My journey of self-exploration, self-discovery, and why things happened the way they did, and why they happened was my personal quest that lead me to face my fears which eventually lead me to my gift, my blessing.

My fear immobilized me. I was stuck and couldn't move past this issue until I received a confirmation through a dream, a dream which I will share with you later in the book. Fear had me so crippled. It was like I was frozen in time and missing out on so much in life. I couldn't move forward in my life until I got past this next challenge. I felt that I was stuck and I knew that I needed to resolve this issue in order to move on. There were many opportunities thrown right in my face. Literally in my face, but fear prevented me from taking that next step, the step that I so badly needed to take. Why am I so fearful? Was it the same old fears of having my heart trampled on again and again, or was it the fear of not being worthy enough to receive love, or the fear of not receiving the love I felt I deserved?

Deep down inside I wanted to know the answer to my quest but yet fear kept appearing and preventing me from moving on. I felt as though I was imprisoned by my own thoughts, doubts, and fears. I knew I needed to find the reason to why my mother disliked me so. I needed to know why she would withhold love from me. What is this purpose? Everything has a reason. My quest was to understand why I would have a mother that withholds love from me. It is to serve a purpose, I'm sure of it. I just need to find out what it is. So began my quest.

Chapter Eight

FIRST LOVE

1 Corinthians 13:13 (King James version) "And now abides faith, hope, love, these three; but the greatest of these is love."

You are the one that saved me. You were my first love. You opened my heart to love. Through you I found unconditional love. You were my angel in disguise; I didn't know it at the time. If it hadn't been for you I don't know where I would be today. You are the one I allowed in. You are the one that opened my heart to love. Because of your love for me I live a life full of love and joy, a life I'm sure I wouldn't have if I hadn't trusted my heart to you.

The love that caused my heart to open and stay open was the love I received from the one I chose as my life-long partner, my husband. We were in our teen years when we fell in love. It was a long courtship and we moved slowly probably because of my issues with trust and with love. How can I trust another; how can I open my heart to love; how can I bare any more pain; how can I do this, this thing called love?

Our courtship wasn't easy at first. I felt like an alien, new to the concept of love and trust. Slowly my heart trusted enough to open, and give love another chance. I was learning to receive and give love. It was all so new and overwhelming at times, it was like an avalanche rolling in. It swept me up and carried me to destinations unknown. At times it even felt like I was being smothered from the weight of the pain that love can cause. My heart would ache and it was hard to breathe. Why did the avalanche of love come pouring down on me? It was so overwhelming and painful at times but I am honored and blessed because of it.

If my partner hadn't opened my heart to receive love, my life wouldn't be what it is today and for that I am so grateful. Hind sight is 20/20 and once I reflect back on my life, it all makes sense of why everything happened the way it did in my life. Everything happens for a reason. I needed to experience those feelings of not being loved, and not trusting others so it would force me to go within and discover my true self. By going within I was able to know myself, my true self, unlock the immense power of love, and see everything through the eyes of love.

My self-discovery process allowed me to get to know who I truly was and what my goals and dreams were; what I wanted out of life, and how I wanted to be treated and how I wanted to live. I knew I wanted to live a life full of love and joy. I didn't want to live a life of fear and anger. I knew I could trust my inner guidance and it was telling me that it was safe to open my heart to love. So I did. I chose love. Love is what we are made of, and love is the coming together of everything to create Heaven here on Earth. By listening to my inner guidance I am now living a life full of love and grace, Heaven here on Earth. The love I feel for others is unconditional and limitless. I have been blessed with an opportunity to see how important love is to one another, for our survival and that is when I decided that I will love all, love everyone unconditionally.

Chapter Nine

EVERYTHING HAPPENS FOR A REASON

Did you ever notice how things play out just perfectly? A certain order of synchronistic events happens and then in the end you think to yourself, oh that's why it all happened the way it did. Picture this for a moment. You are getting ready for work in the morning. You grab your briefcase, your purse, and away you go. Just as you are about to head out the door you look down and notice that you have a run in the brand new panty hose you just put on. So you have to put everything down and then go change into another pair of panty hose. Okay, now you're ready to leave again. You are on your way to work and you are hitting every red light possible. You think to yourself, come on I'm going to be late for work. So as soon as you get through the series of lights you are speeding along trying to make up for lost time. You have quite a bit of time to make up due to all your delays so you are travelling above the speed limit now. You're not the only one that notices that you are speeding. A police officer caught you on his radar and has signaled for you to pull over. You pull over and you go through the regular routine. He asks for your license and ownership, he tells you how fast you were going, and meanwhile you are thinking that you know how fast you were going, and that you don't need an officer to tell you that. You are going to be very late for work. By the time the officer writes up your ticket and hands it to you, you are extremely late now it doesn't matter, so you continue on your route and as you are about to take your exit onto the freeway you notice that you can't enter. Both exits are blocked and you can see why from your point of view, high on top of the overpass. There was a multi-vehicle accident. Ambulance, fire and police have been dispatched and are all just arriving on the scene. It appears that the accident had just happened moments before. You immediately think to yourself, Oh My God that could have been me. Yes, that's right. You were delayed all morning long for that very reason. If you had been on route at the time that you normally would have been, you would have been involved in that multi-vehicle accident that closed off the on ramp and the exit. You shudder to think what might have happened. You see, everything happens for a reason. You were spared that day. There is a plan in place for you and that day was not the day for you to be involved in such a horrible accident.

I'm sure if you look back on some aspects of your life you will see synchronistic events that played a huge role in your life. Everything happens for a reason. I believe that things don't happen just randomly, there is a bigger plan in place. One thing or one experience is leading to another. Perhaps if you hadn't experienced something in your life you wouldn't be prepared for what is to come next.

Chapter Ten

FEAR

*"Let us not look back in anger nor forward in fear,
but around in awareness."* James Thurber

Fear was the biggest obstacle in my life. Fear of opening up,
opening my heart up to others, and the anxiety it caused me.
Fear had me immobilized. I understand now that any hurtful
experiences in my life were obstacles to overcome so that I could
move forward to becoming more of the great magnificent person
I was born to be, that we were all born to be; so too can your
experiences once you are able to change your perspective and look
at situations and challenges with new eyes.

Perhaps you are familiar with the work of art from Kim Jae-
hong who painted a beautiful scenery with a mountainous rocky
landscape reflecting in the water below. An image that when you
look at it differently, from a different perspective, you then notice
that it is an image of a mother and her child praying together.
Much like this image, once I saw things and situations from a

different perspective I was able to conquer my fear and change my life.

I thought I was seeing the complete picture. I was actually only seeing what I've seen before, the types of responses I received before. Once I was open to the idea of expecting a different outcome the fear started to dissolve away. It was a courageous step I took putting my heart out there again, after having it repeatedly broken and trampled on but I knew I had to do this. My dreams had been encouraging me to step forward and swing open the bars that had me imprisoned. Why was I allowing fear to imprison me? A series of dreams and their messages gave me the insight and encouragement to take charge and change my life. I am in charge of my life and I can create the life I deserve. I have within me everything that I would ever need, all the tools and wisdom I need are found within.

I was experiencing many dreams about fears. I would think to myself. Fear? What's that? Why am I having dreams about fears? I'm not afraid of anything, really I'm not. Oh, but I was and I had that fear buried so deep that it took some time for it to surface. Once it did, then all my dreams about fears made perfect sense to me. I had several dreams with different story lines but all with the same message. I was afraid, but of what I wasn't sure. The dream that I will share with you provided me with more insight into what I was so afraid of. This dream in particular is where I was prepared to drive off a cliff and die rather than confront my fears.

The images and the feelings I experienced in this dream were so vivid and are still with me to this day. I believe the reason is because it was a pivotal point for me in my life. It was a very important message for me to receive and it needed to be demonstrated in this way in order to catch my attention.

In my dream I was driving a four door sedan. I was very afraid and running away from something. I was driving the car extremely fast, so fast that everything was a blur. In the dream I recall I had already locked all four doors of the car. I reached back and checked each one again just to double check. When I reached for the back driver's side door I noticed that it was unlocked. I'm thinking how did this happen when I knew I had locked them all? The door was unlocked somehow and I'm becoming even more afraid. Whatever was chasing me was going to try to get in so I'm driving faster and faster with every passing moment. This thing whatever it is, is going to try to reach me. I can't let it. I'm frightened to death and need to out run this thing so I accelerate and increase my speed even more. The car is going very fast. Everything is just a blur, and then all of a sudden the car hops onto a track almost like a roller coaster track made of metal and steel. The track was winding with lots of twists and turns, and sharp bends. I know that I am going too fast and that I could fly off the track at this speed but I keep going faster, and faster, accelerating more and more. The gas pedal is pressed down as far as it could go, pedal to the metal. I am getting a sense that whatever is after me can go as fast as I can. I can't seem to outrun it. I look back behind me and I see someone's right hand and arm reaching in at me. So I continue to press the gas pedal going faster and faster knowing I'm about to fly off the end. I'm going too fast in order to take the next bend and stay on the track. I continue to go full throttle all the while knowing that I could fly off. I do. I am air born and falling towards the ground. It felt like I had just jumped off a cliff. I am still in the car and dropping to the ground at a rapid speed. I know that I will die when I hit the ground, and I have about 3 seconds before I die. I start praying aloud "Lord take me, Lord keep me safe." and just one second before death, I woke up. My heart was racing. I thought it was going to jump out of my chest. My dream was so vivid and powerful that I really felt that I could have died in my dream that night!

So now let's analyze the dream.

A car symbolizes ambition and drive, and ability to navigate through life. Driving the car indicates I am taking an active role in the way my life is going. I am in the drivers' seat of my life.

Running away from whatever was chasing me means that I am avoiding a situation that I think is unconquerable. Or it could mean that I am running away from fear itself. It was my past that I was trying to outrun. My past was trying to reach out and touch me. I was too afraid to go there that's why I was accelerating my vehicle the way that I did. I needed to go faster and faster to avoid my past.

The tracks being windy, and twisting and turning indicates life's ups and downs, twists and turns. When the car suddenly appeared on a track, I believe it indicated I'm on the right track with my life but I'm very fearful of the destination. I'd rather die than confront my past. I don't want to face the pain of my past so I continue at a high rate of speed even if it means death if I do.

The doors of the vehicle symbolize opportunities that are presented before me. I knew exactly what this meant. I had many opportunities to communicate to my parents but they avoided me and so I avoided them. We lived in the same area, and shopped at the same retail stores so we were bound to run into one another once in a while. There were many times we almost collided in doorways of stores. One time they had exited a store and were walking through the doorway when they almost collided with me. They were right there in my face, literally. You can see again, the messages were strong even in my waking life. They were thrown right in my face but I was too afraid to go there. I was too afraid to open that door. That's why in my dream I was making sure all the car doors were locked. They weren't getting in to hurt me again. I wasn't going to let them into my life again, and continue to hurt me the way they always did. I'm locking those doors nice and tight.

Hands represent communication. Someone was trying to reach out to me, to communicate to me. Was it me trying to communicate to myself or was it my parents trying to reach for me? The right hand in particular may also be a pun on words meaning that some decision or something is being made right. A disembodied hand indicates a point of view or being misunderstood.

Death indicates a transitional phase, becoming more enlightened, and more spiritual. It also means self-discovery, a positive development, and an end to the old ways happening in my life. Death is usually a positive symbol, it is an end to the old and big changes are ahead.

We are all here on this wonderful Earth learning, evolving, and becoming more of who we are truly meant to be, a great magnificent being. You have within you everything you will ever need, all the wisdom and tools you need are found within. The big mighty oak is already in the little acorn and so too is your Great Magnificence. Reach down inside and find your inner strength to face your greatest fears. Once I did I soon realized that by overcoming my biggest obstacle which was fear I received the greatest gift of all, a blessing. Hidden within my fear was the gift of love.

PART III

Forgiveness

Chapter Eleven

RECONCILIATION

Strong feelings of being unwanted, unloved, and not included from a very young age, kept me driven to find out why, and it was through that self-discovery when I uncovered the answer to my quest. My dreams were guiding me along the way and giving me validations when I was feeling doubtful. My dreams are what encouraged me to continue on my quest. The messages I received through my dreams drove me to overcome my fear, find forgiveness in the darkest place, and open my heart to love. By journaling and analyzing my dreams I was able to see the diamonds in the treasure chest of my soul. Because it was through dreaming that I was able to allow myself to forgive and by doing so, even more love was shown to me. I had unlocked the immense power of love within and started to see everything through the eyes of love.

It was as though I had graduated in some way. It felt as though I had accomplished something of great importance but my job wasn't quite complete. There is more to this life that I am to accomplish. That was just one aspect, one step. A step that I needed to make in order to take the next steps in life that will be presented before me. I thought I was complete until I received a dream confirming to me that I had just barely touched the surface. Let me share that dream or vision with you now.

In my dream I had to pull back the cover of a swimming pool. The water in the pool was crystal clear, blue in color, and at the end of the pool was a hot tub. The hot tub was churning and bubbling. I was flying horizontally above the pool as I was pulling back the cover. I recall trying to jump in the pool but I couldn't, I just kept flying over it, floating freely and softly above with my toes just barely touching the surface of the water. As much as I tried I couldn't get into the water, just my toes. I remember looking at the hot tub and the churning water and discovered a special magnifying glass that would allow me to see through churning water clearly. It was as if whatever I was looking at through that magnifying glass was crystal clear and anything around it was bubbling and churning. I had perfect insight and vision. I recall thinking that it would be very useful to have, to be able to see things clearly. If a child were under the churning water, I would be able to use my special tool and see them clearly, and be able to pull them up to safety.

In this dream I received the message that I have graduated from just one step, there are more to accomplish. I may have completed just one important step in the journey of my life, one grade but there are many more to come. All my life tasks have not all been completed.

> *"There will come a time when you believe everything is finished. That will be the beginning"*
> Louis L'Amour

The reason I know this is the portion of my dream where my toes were just barely touching the surface. That was my confirmation that I have just barely touched the surface of my healing, my journey has just begun. Toes are symbolic of the way we walk through life either with grace and poise, or the lack thereof. Water is cleansing and symbolic of healing, knowledge and refreshment. Clear calm water as it was in the pool means that I am in tune with my spirituality, and it denotes peace of mind and rejuvenation. Blue represents truth, wisdom, heaven, tranquility, loyalty, and openness. The churning water in the hot tub symbolizes chaos and turmoil.

To summarize my dream I would have to say that I am flying freely through life full of grace and love and can see clearly through the chaos of life. I have within me everything I need, the knowledge, the truth, the wisdom, and openness to remain above the chaos and help those that are in the churning water. Once again my dreams were communicating to me, reassuring me that I was on the right path, pushing me forward when I felt I didn't have the courage. Dreaming allowed me to have the courage to forgive and by doing so I soon discovered the gift.

Once I was able to see the gift, my pain and suffering instantly dissolved. It completely vanished and love took its place. What had replaced my anger and fear was the greatest gift of all, love. Love had replaced the anger and bitterness I had towards my mother, the one whom I thought was hurting or harming me by withholding love was actually giving me the greatest gift of all, love. Love was waiting for me to discover it within the solution of my fear. Sometimes the one that hurts us the most is our greatest teacher. I felt that I had passed the test. I found love where I thought there wasn't any. I found forgiveness where I thought none was needed.

"Forgiveness is the fragrance that the violet sheds on the heel that has crushed it." Mark Twain

47

Through this life of hidden pain and fear and my drive to understand why I have a mother that doesn't show love for me, forced me to continually search for the answer until it revealed itself to me. My mother was capable of showing love for others but with me it was definitely different and this difference was my life purpose. I needed to experience those feelings so that I would search for answers, and once I did, I began to see the gift, the blessing. Because of my mother's gift, I chose to live a life full of love rather than sit and wallow in self-pity and live a life of bitterness and resentment. This gift was one of my diamonds in the treasure chest of my soul. It was so uplifting and exhilarating once I made the complete connection of why things happened the way they did. As I said before, everything happens for a reason and I now understand completely and I am so grateful that I do. This was my huge ah-ha moment.

Now let me tell you more about my relationship with my mother. I had always felt that my mother did not love me. She would show love and affection for my other siblings, nieces and nephews but why was love withheld from me? This was our relationship. I felt very sad and alone as a child but through my dreams and their confirmations I was encouraged to live my life and understand the reasons why this was happening to me. My relationship with my mother didn't improve at all through the years. There were times that I forced a relationship just to keep her in my life but then it got to a point where I had enough. One day I stood up for myself and voiced my feelings. She completely dismissed what I was saying and shut me out of her life for over nine years. Prior to this huge outburst and conflict, several times throughout my life we weren't talking to one another. She always shut me out of her life. It would last two years or three years but never this long, nine years. I still remember that night as though it were just yesterday. We had a huge blow up and I knew that was the end of our relationship. I recall there were several times I cried myself to sleep at night. She had no idea of the pain she had caused me. It was excruciatingly painful for me to have her shut me out of her life in that way. I felt like I was grieving for the loss of a mother that I never had, a mother that I truly longed for. There were times we would bump into one another but if she ever saw me, she'd ignore me and it would be like I was invisible to her even if I was standing within a foot of her. She wouldn't acknowledge me at all. I did not exist in her eyes. So obviously my relationship with my mother was always estranged. I kept trying to resolve our issues and heal our relationship but it just wouldn't happen. I felt that the relationship was purposeful as dysfunctional as it was. What was the purpose of our relationship? This is what I needed to find out.

I believe that our lives are mapped out for us. We have a starting point and a destination point. How we get there varies based on the decisions and choices we make along the way, and this journey is what makes life fun and interesting. These adventures create opportunities for us to learn and grow, and become more of who we are truly meant to be, a great magnificent being. The key is to live your life with purpose, your pre-arranged purpose, the agreement that you made prior to being born. I believe that everyone has a purpose and many lessons to learn while living here on Earth. Through journaling and analyzing my dreams I was able to discover what my life purpose was, and continues to be.

Let me recount the dream that enlightened me regarding my life purpose. As I had mentioned earlier in this book you don't have to have a long detailed dream in order to receive a profound message for yourself. Some of my dreams have been quite lengthy, up to seven or eight pages in length when written in my journal. The dreams are like a story within a story. It's like a puzzle and a mystery to be solved. It is exciting and can be challenging but once you're able to decipher their messages it's like you've solved the mystery. I've had some dreams that were just a little snip-it of an image and yet it had a profound meaning for me. Listen to your intuition, your gut feeling when you are analyzing your dreams. The more you practise analyzing your dreams, the easier it will become in understanding the messages.

I had dreamt that my mother had to get credit at a store for something that she had pre-arranged for. I was with her. I was standing by her side on the right. I don't recall seeing her face or anything, I just had a sense that she was there and I was with her. She was arguing with the store attendant, defending a credit for something that was pre-arranged. Once she had that all settled with the store attendant she wanted to buy a hair straightener to give to me. I thought to myself I don't want a hair straightener. I'm also thinking to myself, she hasn't talked to me in nine years and here she is trying to buy me a hair straightener of all things. I don't want that. I want her love. I had no use for a hair straightener, my hair is poker straight. I remember thinking why would she be trying to give a hair straightener to me? And then I woke up.

Right now you could be thinking that dream wasn't very insightful at all. But you see it was, to me it was very insightful. I've been asking for answers through my dreams for years as to why my mother withholds love from me. Once I was ready to see things differently, that's when the dream was presented to me, not before because I wasn't ready then. The dream came once I was ready to forgive.

While journaling the dream I received its profound message for me. My mother was defending her credit for something that was pre-arranged. I kept thinking to myself, something that was pre-arranged? What could have been pre-arranged? Then it hit me like a ton of bricks. I had that huge ah-ha moment, that big light bulb moment. I believe that this pre-arrangement was an agreement that she and I made prior to me becoming her daughter. I feel that we all have a plan when we are born, a map of our destiny. We have a starting point and an end point. How we get there becomes part of our journey. It doesn't matter which roads we choose to get there, what matters is that we do. I believe that there was a pre-arrangement between my mother and I, between a mother and daughter.

This pre-arrangement was our life path, life purpose, and our contract. I was to be the daughter, she the mother. Her contract was to be a mother withholding love from a child, and that child was me, her daughter. My purpose was to live a life of being withheld a mother's love so that I would be forced to choose between a life of anger and bitterness or a life full of unconditional love. I chose love. This was my test, a test presented to me throughout my whole life. When I could see the love that it took to form a contract of such magnitude, I couldn't help but find love for her. Love is what we are all made of, and love is what sees the love in others. That's when I decided to reach out to her one more time asking her for forgiveness where I thought none was needed.

The pre-arrangement in my dream was the contract between us. My mother trying to reach out to me, trying to connect with me on a personal or a spiritual level by gifting me with a hair straightener was a confirmation to me that she wanted to straighten things out between us. Hair is indicative of attitudes and approach to certain issues. We both needed to change our attitude about our relationship. Things needed to get straightened out. There was a lot of confusion and uncertainty regarding our relationship. The straightener could also mean that she was unable to think straight and now she was offering me an opportunity to straighten things out.

Now you can see how a small tid-bit of a dream can be so profound and life changing. If I hadn't taken the time to journal and analyze my dream I would have missed out on healing a huge aspect of my life. I wouldn't have been blessed with the gift of love from my mother. Once I was able to see things with new eyes and a new perspective that's when our relationship changed.

> *"If you change the way you look at things, the things you look at change."* Dr. Wayne Dyer

I was able to find unconditional love for my mother and that was the day I decided to forgive her and write the letter that changed my life. I needed to change my life and my relationship with her. Fear and self-doubt kept popping up but I needed to heal this part of my life. I needed to take that brave first step towards reconciliation.

I recall hearing a story one time about a psychologist teaching a class about stress management. She was walking around her classroom while holding up a glass of water. Everyone expected her to ask the question is the glass half empty or half full? Instead she asked the class how heavy they think the glass of water is. She heard her students shout out various replies ranging from eight ounces to twenty ounces which would be a good guess considering the size of the glass. Her reply to the group was that the absolute weight doesn't matter. It depends on how long you hold on to it. If you hold it for an hour, you'll have an ache in your arm. If you hold it for a day your arm will feel numb and paralyzed. In each case, the weight of the glass doesn't change but the longer you hold it the heavier it becomes. So too do the stresses and worries in life. They are much like the glass of water. You think about them for a while and nothing happens. Think about them a bit longer and they begin to hurt. If you think about them all day long you are paralyzed and incapable of doing anything. This is exactly how my burden of feeling unloved was weighing heavy on me. It had me immobilized from the weight of it. I had carried this burden far too long. It was time for me to release this weight. I decided to set my glass down.

Looking back now I can see where I had several other dreams that were confirming this same message for me. I needed to set the glass down. In my dreams it wasn't a glass it was always a suitcase or a big bag. I would be dragging this suitcase or bag(s) throughout different levels of a house which represents self and own soul. At times I would see escalators and ride them up and down while I was lugging all this baggage with me. Escalators represent movement in life regarding emotional issues. When I was going up the escalator I was addressing my issues, when I was going down I was regressing or experiencing setbacks. There is more to the dream to analyze but hopefully you can see that even if you journal a dream from two or three years ago you can always receive profound messages that you can apply to your life now.

Once I decided to set my glass down, to leave my baggage behind, I was light and freer to open my heart to love. That was the day I decided to forgive my mother and by opening my heart I unlocked the immense power of love within and I received more love in my life. That was when I truly started to live life, living a life of Heaven here on Earth where love brought me back to her. Sometimes life's experiences and challenges are difficult but the rewards of getting through them are filled with love and grace. Once I was willing to change the way I looked at our relationship, that's when the relationship itself began to change.

Love is the greatest gift of all. Love is the greatest power of the universe and resides within everyone. Love is what we are all made of, and sees love in others. It is through love all things are possible, and it is our coming together of everything that we create Heaven here on Earth.

No longer will I live in a world of a pain and fear. The day I started to really live life and open my heart to give love another chance is when I started to create my own Heaven here on Earth. Through the release of fear and anger I received the greatest gift of all, love.

1 Corinthians 13:13 (King James version) *"And now abides faith, hope, love, these three; but the greatest of these is love."*

"I Remember"
I remember the pain.
I remember the hurt.
I remember the loneliness.
I remember my sadness.

I remember my grief.
I remember my inner guidance.
I remember self-love.
I remember unconditional love.
I remember you.
Do you remember me?

"Your work is to discover your world and then with all your heart give yourself to it" Buddha

PART IV

*Dream Techniques and
Common Dreams*

Chapter Twelve

DREAM RECALL

Now let me give you tips and suggestion to assist you in achieving dream recall so that you can receive vital information, solve conflicts and heal your life. First of all I recommend that you keep a dream journal. You may have several dreams throughout the night, some may be fragmented, others may be interesting stories with lots of dialogue. Keep your dream journal handy by your bed. Write down everything you can remember about your dream no matter how minute it may seem. If you wake at 3am write down the dream immediately. Don't wait until you get up in the morning, the dream may be gone. I find that when you wake from a dream it is best to lay as still as possible. Try to remain in the same position as when you awoke. If you sit up or move, sometimes the dream is completely gone. It's almost like the slightest movement would cause the dream to be erased from our memories. If you do happen to move and the dream is slipping away, try lying back down in the same position as you woke and perhaps it will come back to you. Your dream may be just pieces and fragments, but write those down. Everything is important. Every symbol, every word has meaning and an important message for you.

It's best and easiest to recall a dream if you are well rested. When well rested it is easier to focus on your goal of dream recall and you won't mind quite so much when you wake up at 3 am to record a lengthy dream. I find it quite helpful to drink plenty of water before going to bed. It helps to keep your body hydrated but most importantly your full bladder will more than likely wake you up after approximately 1-1/2 to 2 hours of sleep and that is when you will be in REM sleep. REM stands for rapid eye movement which is when your eyes move back and forth under your eyelids. REM sleep is the deep sleep which is the most restorative part of your sleep. Your mind is being revitalized and emotions are being fine-tuned. If you are awakened during REM sleep you are more likely to recall your dream.

Before falling asleep at night remind yourself that you wish to wake fully from your dreams with total recall. It is possible. Have you ever had an instance where you told yourself that you wanted to wake up by a certain time, and you did? This works in the same manner. Immediately upon awakening lay still and mull over the images and conversations you recall in your dream. Even if you can't recall all of the images or words, write down how you felt. Did you feel afraid? Were you happy? Or did you feel like there is something huge and exciting coming your way? Was it the excitement of anticipation or was it anxiety? Your feelings and emotions may have more insight to the dream than the images you saw.

Learning to recall your dreams takes practise. It's like a new muscle that you need to exercise. The more you try to recall your dreams the more success you will have. Persistence is the key here. You will succeed and eventually you'll remember every dream you have throughout the night or even the ones you have when you lay down for a quick nap. Practise, practise, and practise. Recalling your dreams on a regular basis is exciting and motivating, all the answers to all your questions can be found within the dream.

Your dream mind has access to important information that is specifically designed for you, information that you are looking for, questions that you are asking yourself. You could have some sort of struggle or conflict going on in your life and it can be resolved through dreams. As you continue to recall your dreams not only will answers be revealed to you but you will learn more about yourself, your aspirations, your desires, and your dreams.

Once you've mastered dream recall your life will be changed forever. Any questions you have regarding conflicts and struggles going on in your life will be revealed and answered to you through your dreams. Soon you will discover that by opening your heart to heal your life, life itself begins to unfold exposing more aspects of you that you didn't know existed. You begin to evolve and become more of who you were truly meant to be, a great magnificent being.

Chapter Thirteen

COMMON DREAMS
Republished with Permission From DreamMoods.com

"I'm Flying!"

Flying dreams fall under a category of dreams known as lucid dreams. Lucid dreams occur when you realize that you are dreaming and then take control of the dream. Many dreamers describe the ability to fly in their dreams as an exhilarating, joyful, and liberating experience.

Flying represents control:

If you are flying with ease and are enjoying the scene and landscape below, then it suggests that you are in charge and on top of a situation. You have risen above something. Flying dreams and the ability to control your flight is representative of your own personal sense of power.

Flying represents a new perspective:

When you are flying, you have the ability to look down and get a wider perspective of things. As a result, your flying dream is telling you to look at the broader picture. From your higher vantage point, you can gain a new and different perspective on things.

Flying represents freedom:

Your dream flight may be sending you a message that nothing is impossible; you can be anybody and do anything. Your ability to fly signifies hope, possibilities, reality and freedom of expression. It may also reflect your strong will and is a reminder for you not to give up. Nobody can tell you what you cannot do and accomplish. Such dreams can provide great motivation and renewed sense of freedom.

Flying represents spiritual connection:

In some cases, your flying dream indicates that you have reached a higher spiritual connection. You are growing more in tune with your spirituality and your dream of flight is a reflection of this.

Flying represents escape:

To dream of flying can also function as an escape from the stresses and pressures of your everyday life. Instead of confronting your daily problems, you take flight and try to get away from it all.

Flying represents inflated sense of self.

When you are flying, you may feel like you are a superhero. You feel invincible and undefeatable. Perhaps you think you are better than everyone else and have a tendency to look down on others. After all, when you are flying, you are actually looking down on them.

Conclusion:

When analyzing your flying dream, consider the significance of the the height, direction and speed of your flight. Flying high and/ or fast is analogous to your level of confidence. If you are flying low, then it indicates that you are content with the pace of your current life. Flying backwards implies that you are reminiscing about your past.

Usually a flying dream is described as a positive and exhilarating experience, but if you are feeling fear while flying, then it suggests that you are afraid of new challenge and of success. Perhaps you are not ready to take the next step. Having difficulties staying in flight indicates a lack of power in controlling your own circumstances. Things like power lines, trees, or mountains may be obstacles that you encounter in flight. These obstacles symbolize something or someone who is standing in your way in your waking life. You need to identify what or who is trying to prevent you from moving forward. Difficulty flying may also be an indication of a lack of confidence, lack of motivation or some hesitation on your part. Perhaps you have set unrealistic goals for yourself and now you are struggling to meet those goals.

"I'm Naked!"

So you are going about your normal routine - going to school, waiting for the bus, shopping at the store or just walking down the street - when you suddenly realize that you have forgotten to wear pants or that you are, gasp, buck naked! Dreaming that you are completely or partially naked may be alarming, but is very common. Nudity symbolizes a variety of things depending on your real life situation.

Nudity indicates vulnerability:

When you are without your clothes, you are also most vulnerable. There is absolutely nothing that you can hide behind. Thus the dream may parallel a waking situation where you feel helpless or where you have completely let your guard down. Perhaps you are in a relationship where you have opened yourself up at the risk of getting rejected.

Nudity indicates fear of exposure:

Becoming mortified at the realization that you are naked in a public place may reflect your fear of being exposed and feelings of shame. You may be hiding something and are afraid that others can see right through you. Hence, you dream of yourself naked!

Metaphorically, clothes are a means of concealment. And depending on the type of clothes you wear, you can hide your identity or be someone else. But without your clothes, everything is hanging out for all to see. You are exposed and stripped of your defenses. Thus your naked dream may be telling you that you are trying to be someone who you really are not. You are afraid of being exposed as a fraud or phony. Such anxieties are elevated especially in situations where you are trying to impress others. Perhaps you are in a new work environment or in a new relationship. You may be apprehensive in revealing your true feelings in these situations and are afraid of being ridiculed or disgraced.

Nudity indicates insecurity:

Your naked dream may also point to insecurity issues. You feel that all eyes are always on you - laughing at you, judging you or criticizing you. Being naked magnifies the notion that everyone is pointing at you and laughing. Most of the time, it's all on your head.

Nudity indicates feeling unprepared:

Nudity also symbolizes being caught off guard, not measuring up or not being ready for some important task. Finding yourself naked at work or in a classroom suggests that you feel unprepared for a project at work or school. You fear that some flaw will be brought to public attention. Dreaming of being naked is also an indication that you have set unrealistic goals where you have no way of meeting them.

Nudity indicates arrogance:

Some dreams where you find yourself naked may be pointing to your arrogance in some waking situation. Perhaps you have a tendency to look down on people or think that you are better than others. By stripping you down to your birthday suit, the dream may serve to humble you.

Nudity indicates freedom of expression:

If you dream that you are proud of your nakedness and show no embarrassment or shame, then it symbolizes your unrestricted sense of freedom. You have nothing to hide and are proud of who you are. You are trying to get to the "bare facts." The dream relates to your honesty, openness, and carefree nature.

Nudity indicates attention:

In some cases, dreaming of being in the nude implies that you are looking for attention. You want to get noticed, but are going about it the wrong way. You are drawing the wrong attention to yourself.

Conclusion:

Often times, when you realize that you are naked in your dream, no one else seems to notice. Everyone else in the dream is going about their business without giving a second look at your nakedness. It just reiterates that your concerns or anxieties are your own projections; no one will notice except you. You may be magnifying the situation and making an issue out of nothing.

"I'm Being Chased!"

Being chased in your dream is one of several common dream theme stemming from feelings of anxiety in your waking life. In such dreams, you could be running from an attacker, an animal, a monster or some unknown figure who wants to hurt or possibly kill you. Flee and flight is an instinctive response to a physical threat in the environment. Thus it is natural to run or hide or try to outwit your pursuer.

Being chased signifies avoidance:

To dream that you are being chased is an indication that you are avoiding some issues in your waking life. The actions in your dream exemplify how you respond to pressure and cope with fears, stress or various situations. Instead of confronting the situation, you have a tendency to run away and avoid issues that you are uncomfortable with addressing.

Being chased signifies close-mindedness :

If someone is chasing you in your dream, then it may also refer to your close-mindedness. You are refusing to acknowledge a certain viewpoint or idea and don't even want to give a listen to any opinion that is different from yours.

Being chased signifies running away from yourself :

Another way to analyze your chase dream is how the pursuer or attacker may be an aspect of your own Self. Perhaps you are suppressing or rejecting certain feelings or certain characteristics of your Self. Anger, jealousy, fear, and even love can manifest as a threatening figure in your dream. And you could be projecting these feelings onto the unknown chaser.

Being chased signifies fear :

Running from an attacker in your dream may simply represent your fear of being attacked. Such dreams are more common among women than men, who may feel physically vulnerable in their surroundings. All you have to do is turn on the news to hear stories of violence and sexual assault.

You are the one chasing:

If you are the one doing the chasing, then the dream may highlight your drive and ambition to go after something you want, or go after someone you want. On the other hand, it may also mean that you are falling behind in some aspect of your life and are having to catch up to others.

Conclusion:

In understanding your own dream of being chased, ask yourself who is chasing you so that you can gain a better understanding. What are you running from? Turn around and confront your pursuer and ask them why they are chasing you.

Consider the distance or gap between you and your pursuer. This indicates your closeness to the issue. If the pursuer is gaining on you, then it suggests that the problem is not going to go away. The problem will surround you, until you confront and address it. However, if you are able to widen the gap between your pursuer, then you are able to successfully distance yourself from the problem. In essence, the problem is fading away.

"My Teeth Are Falling!"

Dreams of falling or crumbling teeth are the most common dreams that Dream Moods receives. The typical dream scenarios include having your teeth crumble in your hands, fall out one by one with just a light tap, grow crooked or start to rot. Such dreams are not only horrifying and shocking, but they often leave you with a lasting image throughout the day. So what does it mean?

Falling teeth relates to vanity:

One theory is that dreams about your teeth reflect your anxieties about your appearance and how others perceive you. Your teeth help to convey an image of attractiveness and play an important role in the game of flirtation, whether it is flashing those pearly whites, kissing or necking. Thus, such dreams may stem from a fear of rejection, feeling unattractive, feeling sexually undesirable or from growing older. To support this notion, a dream research found that women in menopause reported a higher frequency of dreams about their teeth. So there seems to be a correlation with getting older and having more teeth dreams.

Teeth are an important feature to your attractiveness and how you are presented to others. Caring about how you look is a natural concern.

Falling teeth relates to communication:

When your teeth is missing, you may also have a harder time talking or annunciating your words. Thus your falling teeth dream may be highlighting some communication issue. You are not speaking up about something or you feel prevented from doing so. Perhaps you are having difficulties expressing yourself or getting your point across.

Falling teeth relates to embarrassment:

Dreaming that your teeth is falling out or rotting may refer to your fears of being embarrassed or making a fool of yourself in some situation. Perhaps you feel unprepared for the task at hand and are afraid of getting ridiculed. These dreams are often an over-exaggeration of your worries and anxieties. In most cases, all your worrying is for nothing. Sometimes what you imagine is far worse than what is the reality.

Falling teeth relates to powerlessness:

Teeth are used to bite, tear, chew and gnaw. In this regard, teeth symbolize power. And the loss of teeth in your dream may be from a sense of powerlessness. Are you lacking power in some current situation? You feel frustrated when your voice is not being heard. You may be experiencing feelings of inferiority and a lack of self-confidence in some situation or relationship in your life. This dream may be an indication that you need to be more assertive and believe in the importance of what you have to say.

Falling teeth relates to health:

In traditional dream interpretation books, dreams of missing or losing teeth pointed to malnutrition or poor diet. This notion may still be applicable to some dreamers. The dream could also be a sign of poor dental health and that you need to visit a dentist.

Falling teeth relates to death:

We don't usually believe that dreams are an omen or a prediction of some future event. However, we have received numerous emails regarding dreams of loose, rotten, falling, or missing teeth and how it indicates that a family member or close friend is very sick or near death. We are including it as a possible meaning of your falling teeth dream and you can decide for yourself.

Falling teeth relates to money:

To dream that your teeth is falling out signifies that there will be money coming to you. This notion is based on the old tooth fairy tale. If you lose a tooth and leave it under the pillow, a tooth fairy would bring you money.

Falling teeth relates to deception:

According to the Chinese, there is a saying that your teeth will fall out if you are telling lies. Thus the dream may imply that you are being untruthful or deceitful about some matter.

Conclusion:

When deciphering your falling teeth dream, look at what is happening in your waking life that could bring about the dream. Teeth dreams may occur when you are in a new relationship, when you switch jobs, or during a transitional period in your life.

"I'm Falling!"

Another very common dream is the dream where you are falling from a cliff, a building, a rooftop, an airplane or from some higher ground. Contrary to a popular myth, you will not actually die if you do not wake up before you hit the ground from the fall. To understand your falling dream, you need to look to what is going on in your waking life.

Falling suggests loss of control:

When you fall, you have no control and have nothing to hold on to. Thus your falling dream is analogous to a situation in your waking life where you are lacking or losing control. You are feeling overwhelmed, perhaps in school, in your work environment, in your home life or maybe in your personal relationship. You have lost your foothold and unable to keep up with the demands of your daily life.

Falling suggests insecurity:

Falling in your dream means you are lacking any sense of security, stability and confidence. You are not sure where you stand in a particular circumstance or in your relationship. Perhaps you are at risk of losing your job or losing your home. Such loss can make you feel that the ground is falling away underneath

71

you. Moreover falling dreams also indicate feelings of shame, inferiority, vulnerability, and/or low self-esteem. You are afraid of not measuring up to others' expectations or to keep up with the status quo. If you have recently have demands placed on you, then it would not be surprising if you dreamt of falling.

Falling suggests reckless behavior:

Your falling dream may be a wake-up call of your reckless behavior or poor decisions. You are headed the wrong way in life. And if you continue on the current path, you are going to hit rock bottom. Falling in your dream could be viewed as an analogy of your fall from grace.

Falling suggests sex:

According to Freudian theory, dreams of falling indicates that you are on the verge of giving in to your sexual urges or impulses. You are lacking indiscretion.

Falling is a result of physiology:

The physiological changes within the body when you "fall asleep" may actually trigger a falling dream. When you dream of falling, you may feel your whole body jerk or twitch. This sudden jolt is known as a myoclonic jerk and is sometimes strong enough to wake you up.

Conclusion:

In order to understand and interpret your falling dream, look at what is happening in your waking life that could bring about the dream. Where in your life do you feel a lost of control? What is causing your insecurities?

"I Failed The Test"

Taking an exam in your dream implies that you are being put to the test or being scrutinized in some area of your waking life. As with most common dream themes, dreams about taking a test have to do with anxiety. In such dreams, you may find that you cannot answer any of the questions on the test, that the test is in some foreign language or that your pencil keeps breaking during the test. Perhaps time is running out and you cannot complete the exam in the allowed time. Or perhaps, you arrive late and miss the exam altogether. These factors all result in you failing the dream test.

Taking a test implies being unprepared:

To dream that you are taking a test suggests that you feel unprepared for some challenge in your waking life. You may even be harboring some guilt because you did not prepare enough for a school exam, meeting, business proposal, or some project. Perhaps you have been procrastinating on a task and waited until the last minute to cram it all in.

Taking a test implies fear of failing:

Sometimes you may be overly anxious about a real life exam, interview, etc. You always think of the worse case scenario. As a result, such anxiety could manifest into a dream where you fail a test. Most of the time, though, people who have such dreams are unlikely to fail a test in real life.

Taking a test implies lack of confidence:

Failing a test in your dream says a lot about your self-esteem and confidence or the lack of. You tend to sell yourself short and overly worry about not making the grade or that you are not measuring up to other people's expectations of you. You may even be described as a people pleaser because you don't want to let others down. You always second-guess yourself and fear not being accepted or not being good enough.

By failing the dream test, you may be expressing a desire to hold yourself back. Perhaps you are not mentally ready to move forward to the next level.

Taking a test implies setting your goals too high:

If you set your goals too high, you may also experience a test taking dream. The dream may be telling you that you are setting yourself up for failure because you have set unrealistic goals for yourself.

Taking a test implies being scrutinized:

Test dreams are also an indication that you are being judged. These dreams serve as a signal for you to examine an aspect of yourself that you may have been neglecting and need to pay more attention to.

Conclusion:

In order to better understand your test taking dream, identify what aspect of your waking life is giving you a lot of anxiety or making you feel inadequate. It is also important to keep in mind that dreams about taking a test are usually never about the content of the test. It is more about the process and about the feelings you experience while taking the test.

Conclusion

Progression can only be made by letting go of what was to make room for what is and yet to be, a prelude to something far richer and far better than I could have ever dreamed. By letting go there is more room to receive and by going within there are solutions and profound insights waiting to be discovered.

No longer do I grieve for the loss of a mother I never had. No longer do I hold high expectations of what our relationship should be. My new perspective has had a profound effect on my life. I know my mother loves me and for that I'm grateful. Perhaps someday I will have a mother who is also my best friend.

My journey has made me more aware of the importance of family, one of God's greatest masterpieces. My dream is a life rich in love, and to be the best mother and a best friend to the two most beautiful girls in the world, my daughters.

May your life be full of love and grace, may you be gifted with many blessings along the way, and may your journey reveal to you the treasures of your soul.

Sending Love and Blessings to All.

> *"When I let go of what I am, I become what I might be"* Lao Tzu

Bibliography

Vigo, Michael. *What's in your Dream?: An A-Z Dream Dictionary.* (2010). Concise Edition

Vigo, Michael. *Your Online Source for Dream Interpretation*s
http://www.dreammoods.com

Greenberg, Dr. Gary: A Grain of Sand: Nature's Secret Wonder
http://www.sandgrains.com/Sand-Grains-Gallery.html

Nacson, Leon. *A Stream of Dreams, The Ultimate Dream Decoder for the 21ˢᵗ Century.* (2004)

Nacson, Leon. *21 Days to Master Decoding Your Dreams.* (2011)

Nacson, Leon. *Interpreting Dreams A-Z.* (1999)

Linn, Denise. *Hidden Power of Dreams, The Mysterious World of Dreams Revealed.* (2009)

Linn, Denise. *Hidden Power of Dreams, How to Use Dreams On Your Spiritual Journey.* (1997)

Wallace, Ian. *The Top 100 Dreams: The Dreams That We All Have and What They Really Mean.* (2011)

MacGregor, Trish. *Complete Dream Dictionary.* (2010)

van der Merwe, Martin. *Hearing God – Dream Dictionary.* (2009)

Crisp, Tony. *Dream Dictionary.* (2007)

Amar, Silvana. *The Bedside Dream Dictionary.* (2007)

Eason, Cassandra. *Modern Book of Dream Interpretation.* (2005)

Dream Journal

Seven steps in keeping a dream journal:

1. Keep a notebook or a journal by your bed ready to write down your thoughts and feelings.
2. When you wake, do not move. Lay there and think about the dream, let it sink in. Recall the feelings you experienced in your dream.
3. Write down your dream before it all starts to fade away even if it's only 3am. You may think that you'll be able to remember it in the morning but it will more than likely all fade away before you get out of bed in the morning.

   Write down every detail, where were you, who was there, what did you see, what were the colors, did you hear conversations, was there a song going through your head just before you woke, and most importantly how did you feel during the dream, and how did you feel when you woke.
4. If you are not able to articulate your dream, draw the image of what you saw.
5. Date your journal entry, and give it a title.
6. Think of how this dream relates to an experience or a situation in your waking life. Can you see parallels? If so, make notation of that.
7. Reference your favourite source of dream interpretation and start analyzing your dream.

Now the fun begins, start analyzing your dreams so you can better understand your life and how to overcome some of life's struggles or challenges. Pick things apart in your dream one item at a time, one color at a time, and then bring it all in together and summarize what you think the dream means to you. If you hear songs playing in your head just before waking, look up the lyrics of that song and analyze that. Good luck and enjoy the adventure!

Date: _____ **Title:** _____

Dream Details:

_____
_____
_____
_____
_____
_____
_____
_____
_____
_____
_____
_____

Dream Analysis:

_____
_____
_____
_____
_____
_____

Date: _____ Title: _____

<u>Dream Details:</u>

_____
_____
_____
_____
_____
_____
_____
_____
_____
_____
_____
_____
_____

<u>Dream Analysis:</u>

_____
_____
_____
_____
_____
_____

Date: _____ **Title:** _____

<u>Dream Details:</u>

_____
_____
_____
_____
_____
_____
_____
_____
_____
_____
_____
_____

<u>Dream Analysis:</u>

_____
_____
_____
_____
_____
_____

Date: _____ **Title:** _____

Dream Details:

_____
_____
_____
_____
_____
_____
_____
_____
_____
_____
_____
_____

Dream Analysis:

_____
_____
_____
_____
_____
_____

Date: _____ **Title:** _____

Dream Details:

_____
_____
_____
_____
_____
_____
_____
_____
_____
_____
_____
_____
_____

Dream Analysis:

_____
_____
_____
_____
_____
_____

Date: ———————————— **Title:** ————————————

<u>Dream Details:</u>

_____

_____

_____

_____

_____

_____

_____

_____

_____

_____

_____

_____

<u>Dream Analysis:</u>

_____

_____

_____

_____

_____

_____

Date: _____ **Title:** _____

Dream Details:

_____
_____
_____
_____
_____
_____
_____
_____
_____
_____
_____
_____

Dream Analysis:

_____
_____
_____
_____
_____
_____

Date: _____ **Title:** _____

<u>Dream Details:</u>

_____
_____
_____
_____
_____
_____
_____
_____
_____
_____
_____
_____

<u>Dream Analysis:</u>

_____
_____
_____
_____
_____
_____

Date: _____ **Title:** _____

<u>Dream Details:</u>

_____
_____
_____
_____
_____
_____
_____
_____
_____
_____
_____
_____

<u>Dream Analysis:</u>

_____
_____
_____
_____
_____
_____

Date: _____ Title: _____

Dream Details:

_____

_____

_____

_____

_____

_____

_____

_____

_____

_____

_____

Dream Analysis:

_____

_____

_____

_____

_____

Date: _____ **Title:** _____

Dream Details:

_____
_____
_____
_____
_____
_____
_____
_____
_____
_____
_____
_____

Dream Analysis:

_____
_____
_____
_____
_____

Date: _____ **Title:** _____

Dream Details:

_____

_____

_____

_____

_____

_____

_____

_____

_____

_____

_____

_____

Dream Analysis:

_____

_____

_____

_____

_____

_____

Date: _____ **Title:** _____

Dream Details:

_____
_____
_____
_____
_____
_____
_____
_____
_____
_____
_____
_____

Dream Analysis:

_____
_____
_____
_____
_____
_____

Date: _____ **Title:** _____

Dream Details:

_____
_____
_____
_____
_____
_____
_____
_____
_____
_____
_____
_____

Dream Analysis:

_____
_____
_____
_____
_____
_____